SPARKS IN THE DARK

Thank you,

Nancy James

Marjorie Wonner

SPARKS IN THE DARK
Poems by Marjorie Wonner

CHERRY GROVE COLLECTIONS

Published by Cherry Grove Collections
P.O. Box 541106
Cincinnati, OH 45254-1106

ISBN: 9781625491503
LCCN: 2015947685

Poetry Editor: Kevin Walzer
Business Editor: Lori Jareo

Visit us on the web at www.cherry-grove.com

ACKNOWLEDGMENTS

Grateful acknowledgment to the following publications in which the following poems appeared.

"A Love Poem" (previously titled "The Avenger"), *2nd Tuesday Anthology*

"At The Lutheran Home" (previously titled "At The Old Folks' Home"), *Time of Singing, A Magazine of Christian Poetry*

"Butterfly," *2nd Tuesday Anthology*

"Casting A Line," *Time of Singing, A Magazine of Christian Poetry*

"Fireflies" (previously titled "Beginnings"), *The Pittsburgh Quarterly*

"Mother's Quarter-Sawn Oak Bed," *Time of Singing, A Magazine of Christian Poetry*

"On Giving Evan The Antique Bulldog Bank," *Time of Singing, A Magazine of Christian Poetry*

"Playing House," *2nd Tuesday Anthology*

"The Watch" (previously titled "The Shepherds Watch"), *The Spoon River Quarterly*

"When I Am An Old Woman," *2nd Tuesday Anthology*

"Winter Of Seventy-Eight," *Dwelling in possibility: Voices of Erie County*

For my grandchildren, Evan and Rachel.
For my children Ginger, Phyllis, Tom and Barb.
For my husband Jack and in memory of my husband Ray.
All have inspired and supported me.

Contents

I

WINTER OF SEVENTY-EIGHT

Ma died that woeful winter, frigid cold
and snow so deep they kept her casket
in a back room until the first spring thaw.

After the funeral I rode home with Dad,
put the flowers in the parlor. They froze.
The beginning of a brooding long winter.

Every day Dad dug a track to the barn,
milked the cows, fed and bedded them,
kept the wood coming and the larder full.

I cooked his meals, washed his overalls,
kept house for him the way you keep
house when you heat only two rooms.

Some doleful days, I pulled on my boots,
waded hip-deep out to the mailbox
hoping someone still remembered me.

During afternoon respite from chores,
we sat beside the window and watched
the animated flurry at the feeder.

Cardinals, jays, nuthatches, juncos
always welcome, always there. One day
late in winter, evening grosbeaks came.

I welcomed their presence as the Dutch
welcome storks in their chimneys, harbingers
of good; birdsong again in the lilacs.

INCOMMUNICADO

I don't beat around the bush. I put it

plain. Lay it on the line. Ask me any

question, you get an answer. Probably

not what you want to hear. I don't tell

white lies. I say it straight or hold my

laconic tongue. Don't ruffle the breeze

with something more foul than unflawed

country air. I enjoy in dazzling silence

the clean scent of newly spread manure.

I don't waste words on things already

better than words. If I am in a room

sitting there, in the dark, and you come

in, don't expect me to speak. The words

in my brain are playing so loud I can't

drown them out with sound. Just sit

serene with me and you'll hear poetry.

THE ASTRONOMY OF LOVE

I would buy you the moon with a fence
around it, you used to say. And I knew
you would if you could, a picket fence

with roses climbing every post.
You said, *I love you,* then asked,
Do I say that too often? I laughed

and answered, "I don't think so.
Who else are you saying it to?"
Don't tease me, you begged.

And I teased you all the more.
When I was cooking in the kitchen
and you wandered through, you told me,

I can't keep my hands from touching you.
I said, "Try the duct tape in your tool box."
The moon is blue tonight, that rare

phenomenon I've never seen before.
It shines through my bedroom window
brighter than the blazing sun at threshing time

in August. I search its shimmering surface
for the fence I know is gone and the roses,
as dead as you have been these thirty years.

MOTHER'S QUARTER-SAWN OAK BED

My love and I sleep in my mother's bed;
in peace we sleep this gentle night in June
and on the floor beside us sleeps Old Red.

My mother, these past twenty years, is dead.
Through our west window shines the silent moon.
My love and I sleep in my mother's bed;

the one my father bought when they were wed.
Down by the lake, I hear a lonely loon
and on the floor beside us sleeps Old Red.

The cat comes down the hall with cautious tread.
On nights like this the morning comes too soon.
My love and I sleep in my mother's bed.

Two are better than one, the preacher said.
We curl into each other spoon to spoon
while on the floor beside us sleeps Old Red.

Now, in my dreams, I smell the rising bread;
tomorrow we'll have toast and jam at noon.
My love and I sleep in my mother's bed
and on the floor beside us sleeps Old Red.

FEBRUARY

Shiny snow muffles our short stretch of road.
A neighbor's car whispers past. An hour
later another car, another whisper.

I take my book and go to the west room
where a February sun shines on the bed.
I linger by the window gazing at the stillness
behind the house, unbroken except for
the tracks of rabbits, raccoon, a stray cat,
a deer running hard between the bank-
barn and a fence line to the east.

I lie in the yellow warmth to read;
and somewhere between turning pages
and dozing off I hear a harness jingle,
I smell the syrupy steam rising over
my father's sugar shanty.

It's been fifty years since Dad last
harnessed horses to a sled and headed out
to tap the trees in his maple grove.
He's been dead thirty.

STAR GAZING

Tonight is the perfect night, Dad said.

He took my hand, led me to the well
behind the house, lifted the plank cover
as Mother did when she lowered
milk to cool.

Look just over the edge, he said
but don't let your head shut out the sky.
Look all the way down.
Do you see those little yellow stars?

He took a pebble, cleaned it on his pants,
dropped it in so I could see the twinkles
in the deep, dark water.

Stretching on skinny, four-year-old legs
leaning over the stone wall
of the kitchen well, I saw the stars
dancing with Dad.

MUMBLETY-PEG

The backhouse door stood ajar
as it usually did; summer sun
streamed in. My brother, thirteen,
more or less, mumblety-pegged his way
along the path, whistling,
flipping his knife into the ground,
pulling it out, flipping again.
That was the summer he mumblety-pegged
all over the farm.

Mother glanced out the kitchen window,
saw vaguely,
went on peeling apples, rolling dough,
not registering the scene
unfolding behind the house
until Dad came in
newspaper in his hand,
big slash in the toe of his shoe,
blood oozing through.

"What did you tell him?" she asked.
"Pull it out," Dad said.

THE ARTIST

She talks with garbled speech, walks splay-legged.

Her arms move in tight, unyielding warp.

Her face is stiff, expressionless.

Children are afraid of her.

She holes up in rented room; carves designs

in sawed-off shelf boards with chisels

from a hardware store, smears on black ink.

Prints on clumsy, homemade press

clear, rich art that flows

without garble, splay or warp.

IT'S A KIND OF PEACE

It's a kind of peace, isn't it
the rocking chair in the inglenook
the gentle heat from the crackling cherry
a book open on your lap.

It's a kind of peace, isn't it
looking through the quiet glass
watching the somnolent snow
falling into soft pillows.

It's a kind of peace, isn't it
the sun slowly disappearing
the solitary lights of a car in the distance
the muffled purr as it passes.

It's a kind of peace isn't it
stars rising in the cool December sky
and having time and introspection enough
to find a meaning in one bright star.

A LOVE POEM

Farm boys dare each other to pee on electric fences.
My teen-aged son and his wire-walking buddies

peed bravado from the tops of water towers in half
the one-horse towns in Southeast Pennsylvania.

My husband, gentle in all other ways, would make
his mark peeing on the graves of infamous villains:

Hitler, Hirohito, Jim Jones, Attila the Hun,
Idi Amin, Vlad the Impaler, and common cads:

an ancestor who kicked his son off the porch
and crippled him for life, another relative, same

blood line, who plowed under his little boy's rag doll,
the step-mother who evicted a nine-year-old girl,

an uncle who sold his wife's piano in the middle
of the night while she was tied in bed; all the men

who ever made their wives beg for grocery money,
those who drank their family's daily bread.

My love would spend the rest of his life peeing
on their graves; and die happy, having avenged all those

quiet helpless people who endured the unendurable.

COUNTRY SLUM

The house was a shack on a concrete slab.
A gray outhouse stood behind it.

Twenty feet north of the house
a tarpaper barn just big enough

for two horses, a cow, and a sow.
A little hay in the loft overhead.

A grain shed leaned against the barn.
A dozen chickens roamed the yard,

scratching in the dirt,
wandering in and out of the house.

Dad talked to the gaunt, unshaven man.
The boy showed me his hunting trophies,

five pelts nailed to the granary wall.
"I'm gonna get five bucks a piece," he said.

The boy was my age; about nine.
I wondered who would give him

twenty-five dollars for the skins
of five barnyard cats.

TO MY HUSBAND IN THE BATHTUB

Our cat is a Pisces. Her ears prick up
when you turn the water on. And when
you have peeled down and sprawl naked

in the tub, when you have adjusted the tap
to a steady drizzle of steam, she comes
to me in the kitchen and coaxes until I go

crack the bathroom door and let her through.
She lies couchant, like the Sphinx at Giza,
on the ledge of your tub engrossed

in the swish of water, the slurp of soap.
Her long tail swings like a metronome,
the white tip dipping, dipping in the water.

A small body brush pops to the surface.
She probes it with a curious paw, pokes
it down. It bounces up. She swats it back

and forth, the way she bats her jingle ball
from side to side, in the bedroom hall.
You, lolling there half asleep, don't know

what a Pisces I am and how like that cat,
I want to sit on the side of your tub,
and bobble anything that floats.

THE HAZARDS OF HUNTING

Four years ago Joe Butler's Morgan mare was shot.
Last year it was Tom Shaffer's Jersey heifer.

Now this red pickup pulls into the barnyard
where Bill Murphy and his boy
stand planning their day's work.

They know that shiny new truck,
it's the city guy who bought the Propeck place.
The guy rolls down his window and yells,

"Hey Bill, look at the mountain goat I found
grazing in your neighbor's meadow.
I got him square between the eyes."

The boy stares into the bed of the truck.
Bill comes over to have a look. There it is—
Sam Porter's blood-soaked billy goat.

Bill leans in and mutters to his boy, "Son,
some people should never, never own a gun."

FALL COLOR

Dusk falls; hunters leave.

Doe staggers through corn stubble

her lips foaming red.

CAROLINA DAWN

The man who turns the sprinklers on
faces east on a distant lawn,
does Tai Chi, like a Cherokee
paying homage to the morning sun.

II

FIREFLIES

Moving china in cardboard cartons
from my house to his, beginning a new life
with a new husband, I see, among the packing
cloths I gave him, tossed askew in the back
of his Pontiac, that dark, drab, wool quilt:
eighty squares of black and gray.

I want to snatch it back, tell him it's too good
to cover furniture. But it was old when I first
saw it forty years ago, discarded already
to the rear seat of the rattly robin's-egg-blue
coupe of my first love.

I remember it, a giant checkerboard
spread under a starry sky, in the middle
of a meadow, moisture seeping through
the batting. The night warm. Mosquitoes
droning, landing on our sweaty skin.
Fireflies ...

The memory comes flooding back, guilt-ridden
still, like the dampness spreading through
my cotton skirt that summer night

MY MOTHER IN A WHITE SILK DRESS

I never saw you in anything as fancy as
that gown you wear in the picture on the piano,
the white slippers, your short hair marcelled.
The mother I knew dressed in common cotton,
pinned her long hair in a bun;
always had an apron on, full of something,
eggs, apples, kindling, clothes pins;
wore mercerized brown stockings, and those
black block-heeled shoes that took you
everywhere, kitchen, garden, church.
You omitted the apron on Sunday.
Wore your one good dress, the blue satin
you made on that treadle machine
when supper was over and lamps were lit.
After you died, and Dad was ninety,
he told me he was head over heels in love
with you when you were seventeen.
Then you moved to Cleveland and he
wrote you a letter every single day until
he wooed you back and married you.

SPRING

Three boys and a girl
in the creek, flipping sticks
at water snakes, always
a sure sign of spring.

The number of boys
may vary, but there must be
the token girl. The boys
showing off, chasing her,

laughing at her screams,
snake dangling
on the fork of a stick.
It's all there but the apple tree.

And some spring when they
turn fifteen they will discover
the orchard in full bloom.

BUTTERFLY
To My Daughter

Cousin Lew has just returned
from twenty years away,
and finds you woman-grown

Why Girl, you turned into a lady,
beautiful and tall, he says, in awed
surprise as though as a child you were

a gray cocoon or striped caterpillar
crawling on some knotted vine
and transformed only lately to this

comely butterfly. But I was there
to see those dainty, golden wings
you wore, a newborn in your bassinet.

DREAM SEQUENCE

Dream One
It is right after high school graduation.
We are in his small bedroom.
I am folding his clothes

placing them one by one
in the suitcase on his narrow bed.
I fold his white shirt,

button it down the front,
fold the sleeves to the back.
I lay the shirt on last, close the suitcase.

I don't know why he is going there,
but Cleveland is only a hundred miles away
and I know he will be back.

Dream Two
I am on a school bus.
I wonder why he is sitting in the rear
three miles past his stop.

I stand to leave and he stands beside me.
Puts his hand on my shoulder,
leans over and kisses me.

I Wake
I always wake from these parting dreams
with that kiss on my lips. Then I remember
he can't come back from death.

CLASS REUNION 2012

The big reunion is next week, classes 1928
through 1950. I'll wear a dress this time.
I riffle through hangers at the Salvation
Army where I buy my clothes, everything
except underwear. It jumps out at me,
long moss-green dress, soft silky material,
size petite. Some slender young thing
with flowing raven hair bought it new,
wore it three times and after everyone
had seen it, couldn't be seen in it again.
So it's waiting for me. I try it on and it fits.
I wear it to the big reunion with my cream-
colored wedding pumps: the only pumps
I ever owned. I sit beside my husband,
class of fifty, and my brother, class of fifty-one.
Three attend from the class of forty-seven:
my best friend, me, and the guy who left
before we graduated. After the meal I leave
the table, head for the restroom, unsteady
in heels and the long dress flapping
around my ankles. On the way back, I feel
my right shoe catch on the floor. I hobble
to my seat, pull off my shoe. The heel
is gone, stuck on the floor, somewhere.

I stay seated all evening. My friend comes
and talks to me. I wave to her brother
and sister. The classmate who quit early
comes over and sits beside me. His eyes
take on a nostalgic glaze. I guess the dress
worn so recently by that black-haired
beauty, casts a spell on him. He looks

at me (Little-Miss-Never-Had-A-Date-
In-Four-Years-Of-High-School) and says,
"You know, when we were kids in school
you were really pretty."

THE SPRING ITCH

The first balmy day in March makes me

want to fling open doors, haul furniture

outside, spread rugs on newborn grass,

scrub floors, wash windows, put up a plank

platform and paper ten-foot walls, makes me

want to shove a piano the length of a parlor,

makes me want to muck out a musty cellar,

sweep down cobwebs, makes me want

to wrest a pot belly stove to a woodshed,

sort boxes of letters in a dark, stuffy attic,

smell the unmistakable aroma of naptha,

have the cry I didn't have when Mother died.

DAVE

One soft summer day a rusty chevy,
full of boisterous boys, roared down
my brother's lane, struck him, head-on.

The brother who painted my cradle pink,
passed me down his childhood toys,
a wicker rocker, crocheted poodle.

The one who roamed the fields with me,
taught me how to curry a horse, milk a cow,
play gin rummy and mumblety-peg.

Shared his college books when I was ten,
showed me Venus and Mars in the evening sky;
paid me buffalo nickels to shine his shoes.

I have nothing left of that soft summer day
but the image of crumpled cars and Dave's
sticky blood soaking into that black-top road.

THE RED BRICK HOUSE

All my childhood I dream that dream; I am looking
at a brick house, arched porch, green ivy everywhere.
The dream bedevils my childhood; the house so real.

I think my brother and I lived in that house. I think
our real family still lives there. I've heard the stories
about my birth, mud so deep my brothers took

the cracky to fetch the doctor, who arrived after
I did; the caul I was born with. I am told how much
my mother wanted a daughter, how joyful my birth,

but the enigma of the house remains; why one
brother and I are adopted and not the others.
I expect our mother to tell us we are adopted.

She never does. I am eighteen and graduate.
A letter comes from Auntie Fae, check enclosed;
train fare to visit her and Uncle George. I go.

They meet me at the depot, drive to their house,
park at the curb. I step out onto the sidewalk;
face to face with a red brick bungalow, porch

with Gothic arch; whole house covered with ivy.
This is my first trip to Chicago since I was three,
when Brother Dave and I spent the summer.

Mother says, after we came home, I refused to
come to her and cried for Auntie Fae a solid week,
before I would let myself be my mother's child again.

FARM BOY IN KOREA

Every time he left his camp
and walked the road to Taegontu
he passed the house of Mamasan.

No matter how fast he strode
her ladies swarmed around,
one sure to fall in step,
strolling by his side, her body
bumping his in even stride.

Her sing-song question
always the same.
Hi GI, You want a short time,
two dollah?
His answer, always the same.
No thanks, I can't today.

She'd say, Why not GI?
Got a glil back home?
He'd say, Yeah, Got a girl.
OK, some othah time, she'd say.
Then she'd drop back
and he'd go on alone.
He didn't have any girl back home.

He was the same GI
who sold his cigarette allotment
to the black market guy,
then donated his ill-gotten income
to the orphanage up the road.

WAR

He is in the kitchen hunting for a knife.

"In the knife drawer," I yell from the living room

where I am pummeling words into a poem.

"It's not here," he calls back.

"Pull out the drawer, and look again," I yell.

The words, sensing diversion, begin to break ranks.

I batter them down, bring them into line again.

"My new carving knife with the black handle."

"I know," I answer, "It's there!"

The words are scrambling wildly now.

"I looked!"

The words rise up in full revolt.

I go to the kitchen, pull open the drawer,

take out the knife.

Stand there knife in hand.

"Did you finish your poem?" he asks.

THE DOG

There he was yesterday, a small black,
mongrel pup loping along my dusty road.

Two hours later, there he was again
wandering down the right lane.

When a car passed, he stopped, turned
full around and watched it trail away.

This morning he sleeps square in the middle.
Cars slow and drive around him.

I'd like to think some guy lost this dog—
took it hunting way too young.

But I've seen too many car doors fly open,
too many little black dogs dumped out

left to wander all alone, no one to say
a kind word, give them a cool drink.

I've seen too many dogs just waiting
where they saw their masters last.

I know how you feel, Little Dog. I've been
through days when I felt dumped out

left to wander all alone, nobody to give
me a drink, open a door and let me in.

Some days I feel like I too, could flop down
in the middle of a road and stare at the sky.

BAD POEMS

Write five bad poems
every day, the teacher says.

Impossible, I think.
Could I let them, even one

live long enough to consume
a sheet of precious paper

when my old white spouse
carries notepads in his pockets

to children in Africa
who have never had paper?

≈

Lost soul that I am

I write in the dark of night

The cry of a loon

III

LOCAL BOY SHOOTS MAN

We didn't have guns when I was young,
I want to tell the world. But that's a lie.
I shot cherry birds when I was eight.
My brother taught me how. The same
brother taught me how to hook a rug.

We all had guns. Every farmer on our road
used one in the dark of night when a weasel
was in the chicken house or a neighbor's dog
was killing sheep; when an animal was injured,
like the blind horse that blundered into the barn
overshot and broke down through.

We shot the hog to be butchered. Some people
just stuck theirs. We shot ours first.
More humane, Dad said.

We shot pheasants, rabbits, woodchucks, deer,
any raccoon in the corn patch between dawn
and dusk. Only rabid raccoons come out in daylight.
One might bite a watchful dog or, God forbid,
a curious child. Death was sure and agonizing.

In truth, we had several guns: a twelve-gauge
shot gun with more kick than Gilbert's mule,
a twenty-two rifle, my older brother's BB gun,
great grandpa's musket hanging over the fireplace.

The only gun we didn't have was a pistol—
a people-shooting gun, but we didn't need one.
We let God or some accident of chance decide

when people ought to die. But even that's a lie.

When we pulled the horsehair plaster
from the whitewashed kitchen wall, we found
the muzzle-loading pistol Grandpa's cousin,
still a boy, had used to kill himself.

GIVING MY GRANDSON
THE ANTIQUE BULLDOG BANK

It's your turn to inherit the bulldog.
Take it in your hands, turn it slowly.
Let your finger follow its curves.

Put your thumbnail into its cracks.
Pet its yellow head.
You'll feel the slender hands

of the grandfather who died
two months before you were born,
the musical hands of a great grandfather.

Put your nose to its nose and smell
the touch of generations of men.
Hold it often; massage your warmth

into its brassy skin so someday
your grandson may find you
in his Davies bulldog bank.

CASTING A LINE

It's setting the clock to go out at dawn.
It's trawling for thoughts with a nylon net,
and it's catching syllables as they spawn.
It's night crawler bait and an alphabet.

It's trawling for thoughts with a nylon net.
It's swatting mosquitoes and casting flies.
It's night crawler bait and an alphabet.
It's rain on your head, and sun in your eyes.

It's swatting mosquitoes and casting flies.
It's egrets and herons and water birds.
It's rain on your head, and sun in your eyes.
It's winding a line and pulling in words.

It's egrets and herons and water birds.
It's reeling in sounds from a stony brook.
It's winding a line and pulling in words.
It's fishing for poetry with a hook.

It's reeling in sounds from a stony brook,
and it's catching syllables as they spawn.
It's fishing for poetry with a hook.
It's setting the clock and rising at dawn.

OUT OF AFRICA

The movie had been everything he promised, the screen
alive with lions on the prowl, zebras grazing the veldt,
fleeing gazelles. Karen and her love weaving

into each other's lives. The poignant dialogue as if
someone were speaking it direct to me, or I were speaking
it to someone else. The moments when there were no

words at all and nothing else existed but the two of them.
That final scene when he flew off and crashed to death
and she read, To An Athlete Dying Young, beside his grave.

My voice was tear-streaked yet, as we sat in a restaurant,
the movie melding with my husband's recent death,
but I found the words to say, such a somber story made me

want a hand to hold. The friend I came with reached
his hands across the table. They lay there waiting, strong,
calloused hands. But to me they looked so soft I yearned

to touch them, take their warmth. But I couldn't make
mine move. It was a long, long silence before I said, I guess
I'm not ready yet. And he took back those gentle hands.

FOLLOWER
after Seamus Heaney

My father walked behind his plow,
His shoulders taut with muscle tone.
His hands gripped tight to handle curve.
He clicked his straining Morgans on.

Surveyor sharp, he eyed each row
And set the coulter straight and true.
He turned the soil in one long roll
As smooth as any baker drew

From steaming stove. He tugged the rein
At furrows' end and dripping team
Came round and round again as long
As there was field and sunlight gleam.

I brought him water in a jar
And sat beside him in the dirt.
Then brought him more and followed him
Until he sat me on his shirt.

So he could press on with his plow.
He told me sit till he came back.
It was no use, I followed in
His steps, my bare feet in his track.

I was the pest, the nuisance then,
Dogging my father to and fro.
Now, he's the one who bothers me
Following everywhere I go.

OPEN HOUSE

My mother held open house
for all the neighborhood outcasts;
a child at our door begging for a pancake,
a lonely bachelor who needed someone
to talk to rainy afternoons,
the battered woman hiding in our parlor
playing Oh Careless Love, day in
and day out on the piano.

I came home from school and found drunks
sleeping on the same rope lounge
where my great-grandmother rested
during the six-day trip to Pennsylvania
in the covered wagon. Dad told their story
so often I could see those God-fearing
newlyweds driving oxen over rutty roads
as clear as I could see that rustic lounge
that never left our living room.

All her married life Mother brought
those derelicts into our home,
let them sleep it off on our family shrine
and sent them back clean and sober
to their Methodist wives.

LESSONS TO LIVE BY

When we climbed the towering spruce in our yard
Dad had climbed it years before; would again if asked.
When we crawled to the top barn window,
he too, had seen that view, Lake Erie ten miles off.
He never said, "Stay out of trees. Don't walk barn beams.
Don't straddle chutes—you might fall through."
He taught us how to shinny up a pole.

And when my brother took a flying leap to the back
of Dad's favorite Morgan mare, and raced her
against a neighbor's horse, and won, Dad was
more proud than angry even though we all knew,
"You don't ride a horse that's plowed all day."
When that same mare slipped on ice and kicked me,
Dad carried me to the house and told Mother,
"Better a broken bone than a broken spirit."

THE CUCUMBER STORY

Stay out of my garden, he says.
If a woman touches a cucumber
it will drop from the vine too soon.
They can tell a woman's hand.

How? I wonder. He never says.
I sneak out in my barn boots.
Pick one; bump into others.
Don't see any dropping.

He doesn't notice. Never says,
What happened in my pickle patch?
Other people have old wives' tales.
I have an old bachelor's fabrications.

THE PREACHER'S TWINS

Fragile bones, thready muscles

scant blood vessels, thin skin

more fish than mammal.

Scrawny, squirming things

too weak to cry.

Little fists not grasping,

eyes unseeing

as day-old kittens.

Born six months

into gestation.

We, in the pews

prayed every day.

Hope died first.

Faith, two days later.

EVE, THE WIDOW SNAKE

who lives these languid summer days
beneath the steps of my front porch

grieving (I think like a widow) —
grieving her serpent spouse, the long
brown snake I met eight springs ago

stretched across my cellar floor
in that lethargic molting rite.
"Kill him," I had screamed,

even though from a child I knew
every snake is a farmer's friend.
My husband carried him out.

These years later, I sense the old
brown snake is dead; I see Eve
by herself in my yard. More lonely

for her mate, I guess, than afraid of me.
She crawls routinely through the crack
in my cellar wall, sheds her skin

where they had always shed
the way, when my husband died,
I moved back to the neighborhood

where we had reared our young.
She returns to my sheltering steps
and I give her permission to lie and mourn

the rest of her days beneath my porch.
It's my feeble atonement for ever wishing
her lover dead. And when my dog

catches her sunning in my front yard
and he would snap her neck
in one quick jerk. I call him off.

NOVEMBER

I want barns full; machinery tarped
and pushed back on the long plank floor.

Clover and alfalfa in the mows, oats in tight
paneled bins, corn shocks leaned against

a wall, the sheller pulled out beside them,
piles of pumpkin. The warmth of animals

wafting up through chutes and cracks.
The smell of cows, horses and sheep;

the grunt of pigs, the cluck of chickens
scratching in the scaffolds, the soft

coo of pigeons in the rafters.
I want barns full this time of year.

IN THE DEEP MIDWINTER

I see you angling homeward

driving your bumble bee

tractor across a Good King

Wenceslaus field, a faggot

of fire wood strapped between

your yellow fender-wings.

Snow on snow lays round about

deep and crisp and even.

Only your tractor track breaks

winter's icy rhythm.

Dear Husband,

If I die someday and you need to write a letter, the envelopes are in the oak secretary. The stamps are in the cup on the buffet and writing paper is in the drawer of the library table.

I don't know who you'll think you'll want to write when I'm gone. In fact, I don't know who you'd call on the telephone, but maybe, the mother of the boy. What boy I don't know, but the day she came for water while you were at work, she said, just tell you she was the mother of the boy. Maybe you'd want to communicate with her.

Maybe Gloria; we see her in the grocery store sometimes, and she always gives you a big hug. Besides, you said you used to think you might like to take her out, before you started going with me, of course. But you might want to share your grief with her. I'm sure she'd be glad to listen.

Maybe it's the one who used to write fancy cards to your mother in the home, and add notes for her to give you. But no, she moved to Oregon. You'd never call that far. Write her letters? No, you told me once, you thought her handwriting showed a certain streak of craziness not compatible with yours.

I give up — I guess I don't know who you'll need to write when I'm gone. Besides, if you're just waiting for me to die to write these hussies -shame on you!
Buy your own stamps and paper.

Signed,

Your wife
(who spoiled you rotten)

PS Please write my cousin in California and tell her I died. She'd want to know.

IV

THE DAY OF THE BROWN THRASHER

I was back living with Dad, doing chores
Mother had done; cooking, not as she did,
but enough to keep us fed. Cleaning,
washing clothes. I kept Dad's life running
as it had for eighty years, plus the five
before he was big enough to milk a cow.

I was churning; butter almost ready.
The latch on the back door lifted.
Come, Dad said. Come and see this
beautiful sight. I followed him out past

the pump, beyond the barn, down the lane
to the half-finished nest in the brush
by the pasture gate. She swung down,
wings rusty red, a slender bird, strands
of witch-black horsetail streaming
from her beak. First brown thrasher
I had ever seen.

I stand beside Dad's open casket; statuary
head and foot, soft lights, Amazing Grace
in the background. Five years, I mothered
my dad who went to the barn at midnight
to milk cows we had already auctioned off.

That brown thrasher still swoops low, black,
horsetail in her beak. And Dad still bids me,
Come, come and see this beautiful sight.

PLAYING HOUSE

One sweet spring when I was five
my friend, Dolores, came to play.
We drank water tea on the lawn,
flowers in blossom all around.

Now fast forward fifty years—

You come home from work today
and find me waiting on your porch.
You greet me with a kiss
and call me, prematurely wife.

I brought a pot of homemade soup,
warmed it on your kitchen stove,
scrounged through cupboards
until I found your last two flowered bowls.

And now we eat outside
mid blossoms of another spring,
and giggle over noodle soup
like children drinking water tea.

BLACKBERRY

betty   buckle   biscuits

cobbler   crunch   compote

crumble   cupcakes   custard

dumplings   duff

fritters   frappe   fresh

grunt   grog   grumble

jelly   jam   juice

marlows   mousse   medleys

muffins   mounds   marmalade

pancakes   parfait   pudding

roly poly

sauce   sorbet   slump

strudel   shortcake   squares

triangles   trifles   tortes

waffles   whips

and all he wants is pie

SUNSET WALK

I walk our dusty country road to the end
of our farm and back to the house,
gauging my stroll to coincide with the sun
sinking into our west woods. I watch

the last rosy glow streak the sky
after the fire-ball of sun is gone.
In the corner of my eye, I catch a blaze
of breath-taking red, as exotic as a Chinese

maiden in full wedding dress—a tree
on a neighbor's east lawn. One tree aflame
against the summer green of maples
and the deeper green of pine and hemlocks.

In the quiet dusk, I cross the neighbor's yard
like Moses drawn to the burning bush. I find
the tree and step into its scarlet splendor.
I wait for God to say, take off your shoes.

And finally, standing under that holy tree
facing west, I discover the source of the aura,
a narrow slashing in the solid forest backdrop;
a missing tree or trees, victim maybe,

of lightning or age, and through that small
vertical slot, the sun still shimmering
with that supernal fire.

AT THE LUTHERAN HOME

Beyond his window pane
three half grown alley cats
dig in the gravel dirt

and seven noisy boys
play kick-the-can
in the parking lot

while Dad sits waiting
in his room with the other
old man who also doesn't know

what day it is
the nurse's name
and why he can't go home.

THE WATCH

The restless sheep huddle in their shed
ready to run at the slightest smell of dog.
We crouch behind the tool room door,
eight feet and a shotgun barrel away,
where we wait for that beast that comes
at night and kills new lambs and slaughters
heavy ewes as they run in the dark, seeking
shelter in a thicket of vines. An old sheep
nickers quietly. She knows he's out there
stealing from tree to tree closer through
the moonless night, watching to catch
an ear as she flees, tear her throat,
rip her belly until her bleeding bowels
spill on the ground.

We'll get him this time. I promise myself
and her. The striped cat springs for a mouse
in the boards behind us. Dad shifts the gun
and leaning forward, peers through shadows
just beyond the catch-pen rails.
I move the unlit flashlight to my other hand.
We're some combination; I'm a woman, fifty,
and Dad, though kindred with his flock
and primed with apprehension, has some
thirty years on me. He stretches full to see,
strains hard to hear. He's gone without sleep
too many nights this week. His head drops
forward, and his hand slips from the gun.
He snores.

The sheep bolt! He's here! He's smelling his way
around the shed. The sheep can't get out this night
to those ensnaring vines, but they scramble
for the door and thrash against the screen we've
drawn across its open frame. I train the flashlight
on the doorway, still unlit but ready.
Anxiously, I poke Dad, prodding him awake.
Is he here? Still half asleep, he speaks out loud.
I nod but he can't see. Is he here? he asks again.
Yes, I whisper hoarsely. The dog flashes around
the corner and off across the pasture, a streak
of dirty gray. The husky tail, curved high,
rides on the wind.
Why, you despicable half-breed wolf, I mutter.

We wait a little longer. Rain starts pounding
on the roof. We gather up our things, blankets,
flashlight, gun. I take Dad's arm and lead him
through the darkness to the house. The dog
will be back tomorrow night and every night
until we shoot him dead.

But tonight we've missed our chance and one
more night's warm sleep. I could have shot him
if I had the gun, I say, as we reach the kitchen door.
He would have tried that screen, I would have got
him sure. Maybe, Dad says, but that's my job.

He stumbles around his collie, sleeping by the stove.
Poor Trix, he sighs, Too old to be of much use.
He bends and pats her deaf, old head and drags
bone-tired to his bed. I go as weary to mine.
It's an hour yet 'til dawn.

AS IT WAS

Once we had a barn, and grandchildren, small
people, who when a day of busy play was done,
sat with us on a quiet lawn in descending dusk

watching bats wing from the hay loft window,
swooping, swirling, mingling with the flickering
lightning bugs; squeaky bat chatter blending

with the constant cricket chirr, mosquito drone.
That was twenty years ago. The barn is gone;
the children grown. We no longer sit in the twilight

in a world where people are swallowed by night,
a night empty, except for flying, creeping creatures;
the hum of life as it was before man came from mud.

ADAM AND EVE

A pair of harlequin
snakes, let's call them
Adam and Eve, crawl
along the cellar sill
working their scaly
length over old green
insulators knocking
them one by one
to the dusty floor, while

they, Adam and Eve,
remain a single entwined
creature with two long thin
necks and beady-eyed
heads rising from their
one conjoined body.

Adam and Eve slip off
the sill sliding, falling
down the concrete
block wall onto the work-
bench, grip its edge
with their fat, shared tail,
drape over the side,
plop down on the floor,
lie there locked
in connubial bliss,

unaware that snakes
don't wed and even more
unaware how transient
is connubial bliss.

TOO SOON

He died too soon, we always hear
when anybody dies.
My brother died at thirty-eight.
I miss his clear, blue eyes.

My husband, who was in his prime
died; void at fifty-five.
I know — I know he died too soon.
I wish he were alive.

My father died at ninety-one
He'd said goodbye that noon.
They gave him tubes and brought him back.
They thought he died too soon.

EROTICA

I am tossing and turning,
tossing and turning,
feeling every wrinkle in our sheets.

I trudge down the hall
to our college son's vacated bed
to let my husband sleep in peace.

Finally, finally I am dropping off.
I feel a presence in the room.
and wake to find him standing naked,

stiff and warm, beside my bed,
He grins his silly, pleading grin.
I open the covers and let him in.

Twenty years later, different house,
different bed, I wake in a semi-trance
and find him standing beside me,

naked to the skin, not even wearing
the clothes we buried him in.
Are you all right? I ask him.

No, I'm so cold, he answers.
Get in bed and I'll warm you, I say.
I open the covers, but he is gone.

BABY IN A BATHTUB

A baby sits in a gray galvanized tub
in front of a gray cross-paneled door, eyes
squinted against a glaring sun. His face

pensive as if he can almost see the future.
Summer drones on. The men bringing in
the second cutting of hay. Women baking

pies in the hot kitchen. A child swats flies.
A maiden aunt minds the baby, takes this
somber picture with a black box camera.

People tell me, write about what you know.
This picture is all I know of my brother, John.

MUSE

My muse keeps me awake

beyond bedtime then steals

into my sleep and swims

the currents of my dreams.

When I awake I am wet

with fecundity. A poem,

some primordial fish, is

beginning to form land-legs.

VOCABULARY WHIZ

my high school yearbook labeled me
and I knew some captivating words
like *pulchritude* and *picayune*.

Even so, my first husband taught me
asinine, a word I'd never heard
and accused him of inventing.

He, I fear, heard it too often
from his mother and his brother.
My mother taught me *felicity*.

Supercilious was the gem
my second husband shared when I
and my arrogant cat moved in.

The cat died. The husband
and I have been together longer
than either of us would have guessed.

Now he's teaching me *nefarious*.
Makes me wonder what
a third husband could teach me.

LAMENT

The gray wind grinds

the northern skies

swallows cry

in a dying elm

the bare field mourns

grain thrashed

and binned in a barn.

V

SACRILEGE

When I was ten Dad told me, It kills a tree
to chop it off and let the sap bleed out.
That's a sacrilege, he said, even though

he had to once in the Great Depression.
Couldn't pay his taxes so he sold Christmas trees
lopped from the tops of his young pine grove.

One miserable day Dad had a tooth pulled.
Paid the dentist with the ten dollar gold piece
his father gave him when he was born.

Told the dentist, Hold this gold coin a week.
I'll be in next Saturday to buy it back.
Saturday the dentist said, It's in the bank.

Dad drove the Model T back home.
Pulled on his boots and went to the barn.
Did evening chores the same as any other day.

ONE OLD FARMER'S SOLUTION TO JUVENILE CRIME

Give a boy a shovel,
let him pitch manure.

Let it be February
when the cows are in the barn
all day and all night
and everything they eat
turns into steaming sludge.

Let the cows be asleep
with their tails in the trench
when he opens the barn door.

Let his back strain
against the shovel weight
until all he feels is ache
and he is saturated
with the stench of wet manure.

Let him carry
water to the house
before he washes,
before he changes his clothes
and eats breakfast.

Let him walk five miles to school.
Maybe then
he will be too tired to hate.

SPARKS IN THE DARK

While Anne Frank was in her attic, writing in her diary,
I was in my cubicle brushing my long black hair,
making sparks in the dark. I knew there were real
sparks made by real bombs in the sky over Europe
and in the quiet before I went to sleep, I listened
to the evening flight leaving Erie, sure that one night
that airplane roar would be the Luftwaffe dropping
bombs on the sanatorium. I was ten, away from home
and scared. In the idle daylight hours, we children
bickered about whose parents would come to get us
when the war broke out in Erie. "Mine will come,"
they each insisted, though theirs never came
on visiting day. Mine came every Sunday,
but it was a year before my heart was well again
and they could take me home. After that,
no one in our house ever mentioned the sanatorium.

MY BIG BROTHER TAUGHT ME

My big brother taught me how to milk Old Bessie,
how to harness Polly and Dick and scuffle a field,

how to tell an oak from an ash, a soft maple from a hard maple,
how to pull a crosscut saw and stack firewood.

My big brother taught me how to load a gun and shoot cherry birds;
how to play gin rummy while the sap was boiling down.

He taught me how to play Old Black Joe on the xylophone,
how to whistle through my thumbs.

He showed me constellations in the sky, the bears, the goat, a ram.
He taught me how to bake banana bread, and hook a rug.

When I was old enough he taught me how to drive a car.
But I had to learn by myself how to grieve when he died.

DARK WINTER

You die

in the middle of a long, dark winter

and I stumble numbly

through the cold death leaves

until at last it's spring

and I rejoice to find

that life goes on.

But then I wake one day

to find snow sliced

across new grass

and I'm surprised to learn

my thawing body grieves.

READING TOMBSTONES BY FLASHLIGHT
Bennington, Vermont   October 1997

There is no moon. The stars are pinholes
in the blanket of black sky.

The frosty steeple light of the old First Church
casts undulating shadows across the rows
of stark, white stones.

On the Reverend Mr Jedidiah Dewey's stone
two roosters raise an immortal crown
over a winged death's head.

Sarah Hubbell 1792 The amiable Consort
of Lieu Aaron Hubbell died in the 31st
year of her life. Oh Relentless Death

The angel of death for James Breckinridge
is pop-eyed and bald.   Memento Mori

Mr John Pratt died May ye 16th 1768.
His death angel wears a wig.

We walk in flashlight glow, reading
epitaphs of babies dead, too young to name;
New England women, consorts and relicts,

always amiable. Called home too soon.
Their menfolk as indomitable as the rock
beneath their star-crossed town.

The men of Bennington killed in the battle
etched on the front of a tall, marble stone.

The Hessians line a side panel. On the back
alone, the epitaph of the executed Tory.

The Puritan fathers lie patiently, sleeping
in Christ. Beside them lies the Poet Frost,
his quarreling days over.

PETTY ARSON

The wall of an old workshop, lying
on the ground, the boards worn smooth,
was a great place to play marbles,
jacks, hop-scotch, Chinese checkers.

The kids we were, my brother and I,
played on our wooden platform hours
at a time, until the day we found
the galvanized washtub, dragged it

to our make-shift floor, filled it
with sticks, lit it with the match
my brother, by some stroke of luck,
found lodged in his back pocket.

I was sitting around a table one day
with six intelligent, mature men
and someone mentioned the fire
he had started under the corn crib.

And they were off. Every one had
set a fire once. Two of them
wore overalls and plaid work shirts.
I could see farm boys lighting a fire.

But the guy with the suit and the tie
was a big surprise. Then, they looked
at me, the quiet, gray-haired woman.
It was my brother's match, I said.

MANGE

A grocery sign hangs creaking in the wind.

The door swings with a shriek and a bang.

The church down the street is starker still;

no pastor, no parishioner, no Sunday School pupil,

no tending the needs of the sick, soothing hurts,

calming dreads, cooling angers.

As far as eye can see no stable habitation;

only ghosts of an old neighborhood,

a soup pantry on a muddy lot,

the ubiquitous mall

where gangs have altercations

and the weak stab the weaker.

THERE'S A LOOM IN MY CELLAR,
five feet long, five wide, six high,

built by a carpenter in 1844,

for three dollars and twenty-five cents.

The loom my great grandmother shuttled,

weaving the flax she hackled and retted,

and wool she carded and spun.

Stands as sturdy and ready as ever,

in case I need to weave a blanket.

The round oak table with lion-claw feet,

where I take all my meals, the one

Grandma set up house-keeping with.

Her china closet in my kitchen

still full of Wedgwood blue.

The bed I sleep on every night,

my father's wedding gift to my mother.

That spool cradle in the attic now,

rocked my grandfather, my father,

my brothers and my babies.

The essence of the people who made me

who I am is still there in this wood

and willowware.

THE BARDS WORE BLACK
At The Colgate Writer's Conference

Like penguins at a party,
like Turkish women doing laundry,
these poets all wear black;
the middle-aged scholars in black suits,
their hair dyed black,
black shirted college boys everywhere,
the women, professors and students,
in velvet to their ankles, or denim
but always black, black stockings, black shoes.

I'm seventy. I remember the little black dress
for church and funerals and fancy dances.
Every woman had one.
And the men, used car salesmen, undertakers,
and rabbis wore black.

I don't own black clothes; never did.
I'm a barnyard duck in a drift
of exotic black swans.

PENNY POSTCARD

I read that postcard
in a study hall in 1944.
One classmate, visiting
his sister in Pittsburgh,
wrote the card to another
and that other circulated
it among everyone
in that study hall.
It just happened
to land in my hand.
I remember the words,
the silly tormenting words
of teenage boys.
"Hi, my old buddy, old buddy,
How are things back there?
Are you having fun with all
those sophomore girls?
Save one for me."
And he named a girl. "Even her,
if all the other girls are taken."
The girl he named was youngest
in the class, skinny and shy,

a joke among the boys.

"You ask her for a date."

"No, you ask her for a date."

After graduation

the postcard writer moved

to California, and lived

in the Silicon Valley.

The other guy never

left his hometown.

The old buddy-buddies

got together every few years

at class reunions;

same class clowns

kidding each other.

After graduation

still skinny, still shy,

I was lucky enough to marry

the hometown guy.

A RAG LAMENT

Whatever happened to rags —
dust rags, dish rags, scrub rags, rug rags,
rags to curl hair, rags to make a quilt?

Whatever happened to holey sheets,
worn out nightshirts, old BVDs, pieces
of linen, patches of cotton, remnants

of wool, scraps of flannel, muslin,
gauze; fragments of worn cloth. The kind
our mothers saved for mopping floors,

scrubbing walls, dusting pianos.
drying lamp chimneys and new lambs,
making kite tails, wrapping wounds,

shining shoes, polishing windows,
wiping spills and runny noses, straining
milk or jelly juices, cleaning spark plugs?

Why don't we ever see that row of rags
on a clothesline. Whatever happened
to the rag picker and his old nag, Nellie?

MAN AND METER

An old man

leaning against

a parking meter

says more

about time

than either

man or meter

could.

WHEN I AM AN OLD WOMAN

I'll wear dungarees.

I won't mind if they're patched

and I won't care if anyone else minds.

I'll wear black barn boots out in the rain,

slosh around the yard

because I really like rain.

I might take off the boots and go barefoot.

I might put on a bathing suit

and let the rain slither down my skin.

Maybe I won't bother with the bathing suit.

People will say, "There's a loony old woman

cavorting naked in the rain."

I'll say, "Who are you calling old?"

CPSIA information can be obtained at www.ICGtesting.com
Printed in the USA
BVOW08s1720030915

415600BV00001B/5/P

The sparks of darkness, and in darkness, in Marjorie Wonner's collection remind us that memory is as vivid as life itself, and always with us, good and bad.

"Early in her delightful debut collection, Marjorie Wonner proclaims, 'I say it straight,' and thankfully she keeps her promise in poem after poem. In a plain spoken voice, she tells of the past—a long-ago childhood; a dead husband and a second husband; a country way of living rich in bodily expression and sensual, even sexual, delight; all the earthly relics that make a sacred thing of our living. Wonner's sense of scene and closure, of insight and searching, is impeccable, truly extraordinary, filled with wisdom and the truth that some things can't be figured out, set right, but they can be told with precision, with humor and grief, with the kind of candor that brightens memory's dark corners."

—Todd Davis

"Marjorie Wonner's *Sparks in the Dark* brims with the home-grown knowledge of someone who has lived well, and whose many years of farm life have taught her one of poetry's essential lessons: 'don't waste words on things already/better than words.' Marjorie Wonner's poems let those things—a quarter-sawn oak bed, the brutal cold of a long winter, a brown thrasher, a black dog abandoned on a country road, a pair of mating snakes—speak for themselves in some of the cleanest, no frills writing to be found. These poems love the world as it is, with all its misfortunes and suffering, rather than how we might like it to be. I love the honesty of these poems, their wonderful way of never saying too much; and I love the way our daily lives come alive in these poems. Marjorie Wonner's poems are more than 'sparks in the dark'; they keep a vigilant fire throughout the night."

—Robert Cording

"Wonner's range dazzles, running the gamut from elegaic to comic, reverent to brassy, stark to lavish. But what will stay with me deepest is every poem's plainspoken beauty and this poet's courageous honesty. A wonderful first book."

—Ann Pancake

Marjorie Wonner has been published in *Spoon River Quarterly, Pittsburgh Quarterly, Time Of Singing, Second Tuesday Anthology,* and numerous other journals.

Cover art: "Milky Way," Lee Steadman

Cherry Grove Collections

ISBN 978-1-62549-150-3

90000

9 781625 491503

CHRISTOPHER SALERNO

2013 Georgetown Review Press Poetry Prize Winner